canvas

GROUP MEMBER EXPERIENCE GUIDE

MYSTERY

SERENDIPITY®
H O U S E

CANVAS – Prime • Stretch • Impact™
CANVAS 2/: Mystery Experience Guide
© 2007 Serendipity House

Published by Serendipity House Publishers, Nashville, Tennessee in partnership with Refined Inc., Nashville, Tennessee.

ISBN: 1-5749-4418-5
13-Digit ISBN: 978-1-5749-4418-1

Dewey Decimal Classification: 248.834
Subject Headings: SPIRITUAL LIFE/TRUTH

To purchase CANVAS resources:

> ORDER ONLINE at www.SerendipityHouse.com
> WRITE Serendipity House, 117 10th Avenue North, Nashville, TN 37234
> FAX (615) 277-8181
> PHONE (800) 525-9563

CANVAS 2/: MYSTERY RESOURCES:

- CANVAS Kit (DVD-A, DVD-B, and Manual) ISBN: 978-1-5749-4417-4
- Mystery Experience Guide ISBN: 978-1-5749-4418-1
- Mystery Media Downloads/www.serendipityhouse.com

1/6 In Pursuit	4/6 White Out
2/6 Unpack	5/6 Not Yet
3/6 More	6/6 Follow You Thing

1-800-525-9563 • www.SerendipityHouse.com

Printed in the United States of America
14 12 11 10 09 08 07   1 2 3 4 5 6 7 8 9 10

CONTENTS

The Canvas Setting

Each CANVAS setting uses five different elements to move us into a greater understanding about how God has been at work in our lives and will continue to reveal Himself to us. CANVAS settings move our stories from our hearts and minds into the group conversation. Each setting frames the small-group conversation within a biblical context and helps small groups achieve redemptive community.

Frame In the process of creating a work of art, the canvas first must be framed. Boundaries and context are established as the canvas is stretched over the frame. This part of your time together will establish context, introduce the topic, and add voice.

Prime In the painting process, priming prepares the canvas for paint. Before the artist sketches or applies the first hint of color to the canvas, the canvas must be prepared. In CANVAS, priming includes a short film and engages you at a deeper level of story.

Sketch The artist will sometimes sketch faint lines on the canvas to begin the journey to full image and color. At this point, the subject begins to take shape as the canvas loses its emptiness and accepts the first inclinations of form. This part of your experience will draw elements of your story into the conversation.

Stretch God's broad story of redemption stretches beyond us. He allows certain events to "bubble up" in our lives so that we may know more about Him and about ourselves. Jesus came to set free the captives; to replace ashes with beauty; to bind-up broken hearts. Our lives stretch into the redemptive mission that Jesus continues to fulfill. Here you will be asked to look deep into your own story to find those places where God is at work to advance His art — you.

Gloss Glossing draws out and embellishes the color of art. Framing, priming, sketching, and stretching all culminate here. The Gloss element reveals the way our individual stories speak into the larger story that began prior to Genesis 1:1.

The Bridge

The Bridge element takes you from one CANVAS setting to the next. This element of your experience may be used to get together between each setting, as optional get-togethers, as individual enrichment activities, or as a regular feature. Layers, Treatments, and Stills comprise the Bridges of each CANVAS experience.

Stills   Stills ask you to respond. This Bridge may include journal experiences, directed prayers, or questions to take to God or to your own heart.

Treatments   Treatments are group experiences. These experiences may amount to "dinner and a movie" nights with probing questions and conversation pieces generated by the film or just a time to get together for the sake of community.

Layers   Layers are individual moments of reflection and prayer. Layers will either look back to the preceding setting or forward to the next. Layers are designed to open your mind and heart for hearing God as He speaks to you in the deepest places.

CANVAS Pieces

Throughout the CANVAS experience we've included **conversation pieces** called CANVAS Pieces. CANVAS Pieces are voices that come from various communities and walks of life around the nation. These sidebar comments contribute to the story in their own authentic way, and their presence adds another level to the conversation. As God reveals Himself to you throughout this experience, you'll see how He is at work in the lives of Audra, Daniel, Brian, Mary Ann, and Barry. Each setting begins with a piece of their stories.

Prime • Stretch • Impact

The language of story is the language of the heart. Ecclesiastes 3:11 suggests to us that we are pre-wired to recognize the greatest story — the story of God's plan of redemption — as it is lived out in the world around us. Because life is typically lived between the moments, it becomes necessary to be intentional in capturing the pieces of our own stories. We must look for moments when the story God is revealing in us coincides with the greatest story — the epic story — the story of Scripture. We are called into this story.

CANVAS is a means for drawing your story into the small-group space. It is true that you have an integral role to play in the epic adventure. It's not because you deserve it or because of anything you've done, but because God has invited you into the adventure. At one point in *The Lord of the Rings* trilogy, Sam says to Frodo, "I wonder what sort of tale we've fallen into." With this simple thought Sam is acknowledging what we all feel — that there is something else; something greater than the reality we have known. Sam is alive in the knowledge that we find ourselves in the midst of something grand. These moments present us with opportunities. Each life is an empty canvas awaiting the first color splashes of life.

Using the power of story, CANVAS brings a new dimension to Bible study and draws what is deepest and truest about you onto the canvas of God's redemptive story. The CANVAS experience provides the context, texture, and materials for the journey. Through your story, your experiences, and the colors of your reality, God works to bring your role in the larger story to light.

CANVAS host, PETE WILSON, will be our guide through these mysteries. During each setting Pete will introduce some of the concepts and questions that you'll be exploring during your time together.

Pete is the founding and senior pastor of Cross Point Community Church in Nashville, Tennessee. Pete attended Southern Seminary, and his desire is to see churches become radically devoted to Christ, irrevocably committed to one another, and relentlessly dedicated to reaching those outside God's family. He is married to Brandi Wilson, and they have three boys — Jett, age 6; Gage, age 3; and Brewer, age 1.

Audra   I work at least twelve hours a day after which I cook, clean, workout (not necessarily in that order), and fall exhaustedly into bed. Occasionally I force myself to hit a cool concert or downtown happening, just to reassure myself that I am not becoming one of the "boring married people" the slowly-disappearing sitcoms used to mock with abandon. I've moved five times in the last seven years, most recently making the trek with my husband from Texas to Wisconsin. While adjusting to the bitter Midwestern weather has been a challenge, I have discovered it creates a great excuse for subscribing to Netflix® and for purchasing pathetic numbers of coats and overpriced anti-aging moisturizing products.

Barry   I'm the kinda guy who has to know the "why" behind the "what." Most of my journey following Christ early on was a list of dos and don'ts. People just told me what to do. But these last few years of understanding the "why" behind everything...well, it's just blown my socks off! The pursuit of understanding the why behind my relationship with God opens up not only my will to follow Him, but it opens up my heart to love Him. That kind of relationship is dynamic—not static! Yuck! I hate it when things stay the same. My mind never stops thinking of new ways to do anything. I love to be in a constant flux of change (in some way or another). I guess that's why I tousle my hair... and color it... and texture it. Hey, a little controlled chaos never hurt anybody, right? I'm not a rebel—just a maverick, and there's a big difference. Rebels try to undermine authority, and that's not me. I know who I am, and I know where my place is. Mavericks make good messes because they refuse to be told what to do without asking why they're doing it.

Daniel   I'm a 24 year old raised in church my entire life. I feel like I've been around the "knowledge" of Christianity so long that I can jump in any conversation and debate. While that sounds all fun and good, I'm really just at a point where I want make every decision of my life based off of my love for Jesus. Looking at the Bible to connect the dots of how that looks today is difficult, but honestly I just enjoy the process. The coolest things that I've done recently to connect those dots include coaching little league baseball for the first time, started writing more, and leading kids at my church. I'm typically a pretty impatient guy, which naturally causes me to wonder why on earth God places me in certain situations, but I love to look back on my roller coaster ride of a life and thank God for the adventure.

Mary Ann   Prone to bursts of enthusiasm, I tend to start more than I finish. Though the association stings, my friends often peg me as the one most likely to play devil's advocate. Despite the fact that I enjoy lots of biography, this little blurb has me fumbling around. When I'm not chauffeuring two tweens all over the county to various venues, I'm working on a graduate degree and teaching. I'm navigating life as a single person for the first time in my adult life. Lately I find myself at lots of games and concerts or up early reading anything but what I've been assigned. I love conversing with total strangers, a trait that endears me to some but really embarrasses my children. I can't help but be intrigued by all the peculiar treasures God has put in my path.

Brian   For most of my life I've been a huge sports fan and college football has been my most recent passion. But recently God has revealed to me that something I thought was so harmless has been no less an addiction and method for coping and avoidance than some of the worst of social ills that plague us. So I'm trying to do less of that. I grew up in Kentucky, but love the mountains of Colorado. That's where I feel most alive. The air is so electric and it feels so good to feel it all around. I've come to appreciate relationships more and more, marriage only gets richer and richer, and watching my children move into the teen years has been fascinating. It's a challenge for me to put away the destination for the sake of the journey ... but it's certainly a noble struggle. The story is the thing.

THE MYSTERY OF FORGIVENESS

FRAME

Forgiveness is a concept that is often discussed but rarely understood. It is difficult enough for us to get our minds around the subject when we are talking about human forgiveness, but when we start to think about God's forgiveness it moves into the world of the unseen where spiritual battles are fought on our behalf.

While we may know that we desperately need His forgiveness, it is impossible for us to fathom the great depth of that need. The mystery of forgiveness finds its mystery here in the depth and profound nature of Who God is. We also can't help but wonder how something so valuable can come so freely. Surely there are some hoops we must jump through, some actions we must perform in order to merit this gift. Then there is the realization that coming to grips with God's forgiveness seems to determine whether we get stuck in old patterns or move forward in our life journey. It is these mysterious aspects that we want to penetrate our hearts during this setting.

1 HOW DO YOU DEFINE "FORGIVENESS"?

2 HOW DOES YOUR DEFINITION AFFECT HOW YOU VIEW GOD'S GIFT OF FORGIVENESS TO YOU AND HOW, OR IF, YOU RECEIVE IT?

CANVAS

Accepting God's forgiveness isn't hard. Extending that same grace to others is a little more difficult. Unfortunately, holding on to unforgiveness is like walking a 130-pound, out of control Rottweiler. It pulls and strains so hard against that lead that eventually it controls your direction. And trust me, that direction is never positive.

I've been walking a big, bad dog for several years. I want to let go and release all the hurt and pain associated with a first marriage gone terribly wrong, but for some reason, bits and pieces of unforgiveness still linger in my heart.

Sure, I know we are supposed to forgive. I know I should just say "it's over," "goodbye," and "I forgive you for all the vicious things that were said." But honestly, I'm not completely there. Sometimes I think I am, then something comes up and triggers a nasty response and I realize. . . I'm still walking the dog.

— AUDRA —

PRIME

«‹Show Video 1/6, In Pursuit›»

1. Pete talks about possessing something that brings you an incredible sense of joy. What is that for you? What made it so special?

2. Can you relate to the longing, the desperation, in the parables Pete mentions?

3. Watch the progressive emotions on the mother's face. Describe her emotional condition at various points in the drama. What does "In Pursuit" suggest about God's emotions?

4. Why do you think for some people it's hard to believe that God has an "all points search" out for them? Do you believe God can have a single-minded obsession with you?

5. Pete refers to our place in the "larger story." How and where do you think we fit into God's Larger Story?

6. God is in pursuit of us. How do you think this is associated with forgiveness?

7. At one point Pete says that God is a jealous God longing for the love of His people. He adds that He is a heartbroken God. How do these terms contribute to the mysteriousness of deep forgiveness?

The Larger Story includes God's pursuit of us throughout human history. The gospel begins early in Genesis as God's plan of forgiveness and restoration takes shape, while the Larger Story He is revealing begins long before Genesis with original harmony, then betrayal, before finally chaos and rebellion. The mystery of forgiveness is a narrative that weaves in and out of our collective stories.

SKETCH

The Lion, the Witch and the Wardrobe by C.S. Lewis upholds the literary theory that the greatest truth can be communicated by good fiction. A major character in this tale is Edmund, a boy who is consumed by jealousy for his siblings and harbors a strong sense of greed. When Edmund's selfish ambition blinds him to the power of evil, he becomes a traitor to his own family and threatens the future peace of a nation as well. He is only restored to his concerned brother and sisters after the White Witch secretly negotiates a pact with Aslan, the great lion. Taking the place of Edmund, who is now rightfully owned by the evil of the Witch, Aslan agrees to forfeit his own life in order to appease the laws of "deep magic" which govern the world of Narnia. It is the scene of the mighty Aslan willingly subjecting himself to the taunts and torture of evil that we see the closest parallels between Lewis' creation and the gospel story that holds forth the possibility of transforming our own journey.

It's not okay.

I forgive you.

I took me a long time to realize that I could say both of those things in the same breath and mean them. For years, I thought to forgive meant to say, "Its okay." "Okay" meant things got back on track... but there was always the remnant... the little piece of hurt that I could tuck away for next time. Jesus taught us to ask for forgiveness as we forgive those who hurt us. It's hard to ask for God's forgiveness when I know I don't forgive others so completely. When He offers forgiveness, it is free from all conditions, from footnotes. He doesn't ask for proof that we will never sin again. Unlike me, God doesn't offer forgiveness and then distance Himself to keep from getting hurt. He invites me closer.

– MARY ANN –

It often seems unfair that God would not step in and change some situations that I've been through, and am currently going through. At the same time, I can be confident that His perception of things is hardly the same as mine. I wonder if a caterpillar ever wishes God would make it easier to break out of a cocoon? The ending to that struggle would not be the same if He did.

– DANIEL –

No matter our age, I think there is still a part of us that wants to define fairness like we did when we were 5, when fair meant equal; "even Steven." We were created in His image. That doesn't mean God is just a bigger version of us. He has so much more to reveal about Himself to us.

– MARY ANN –

"According to the law almost everything is purified with blood, and without the shedding of blood there is no forgiveness."

HEBREWS 9:22

---

1. Read Hebrews 9:22. Why do you think God established in Hebrew law the need for a forgiveness ritual?

14Just as Moses lifted up the snake in the wilderness, so the Son of Man must be lifted up, 15so that everyone who believes in Him will have eternal life.   *JOHN 3:14-15*

---

2. Just prior to John 3:16, Jesus' sacrifice is compared to an old tradition. What do you think this says about the "deep magic" of forgiveness?

3. Why do you think Jesus chose not to suspend the "deep magic" and respond as those who told Him to save Himself and take Himself down off the cross by doing just that (Matthew 27:39-40)?

Edmund's temptation began with an invitation from the White Witch to enjoy some sugary confections, but it ended up exposing his inner weaknesses to a degree that even he couldn't have imagined.

4. How do our weaknesses trip us up and work against the sort of deep magic Jesus chose to embrace?

God doesn't love us despite our messes, He loves us because of our messes. The Psalmist says that He remembers our frames and knows that we are dust. The outright forgiveness that we own results from a deep supernatural element that allows us to be whole and healthy. This takes place somewhere within the recesses of our being.

STRETCH

The story of God's forgiveness is the neverending story. Even in heaven we will continue to learn more about the heart of God given that, as finite beings, we will never possess an infinite understanding. So a large part of the mystery of forgiveness lies in its infinity. It's the story that never ends.

"You know the story of how Adam landed us in the dilemma we're in — first sin, then death, and no one exempt from either sin or death. That sin disturbed relations with God in everything and everyone, but the extent of the disturbance was not clear until God spelled it out in detail to Moses. So death, this huge abyss separating us from God, dominated the landscape from Adam to Moses. Even those who didn't sin precisely as Adam did by disobeying a specific command of God still had to experience this termination of life, this separation from God." ROMANS 5:12-14A (MSG)

---

1.   Look closely at Romans 5:12-14 above. What if the story stopped here and all of humanity was doomed to inherit the brokenness of our ancestors without any alternative? How would you feel toward a god who designed that kind of world?

"But Adam, who got us into this, also points ahead to the One who will get us out of it. Yet the rescuing gift is not exactly parallel to the death-dealing sin. If one man's sin put crowds of people at the dead-end abyss of separation from God, just think what God's gift poured through one man, Jesus Christ, will do!" ROMANS 5:14B-15 (MSG)

2. How does God's response to Adam's choice make you feel toward God? What does God's response mean for you personally?

3. In some ways, this type of logic appeals to our modern sense of justice that the sin of the "first man" (Adam) could be countered by the gift of the "second man" (Jesus Christ). So why do you think Paul argues that "the rescuing gift is not exactly parallel to the death-dealing sin"?

4. At what times has God seemed unfair, or unwilling to intervene, for you personally?

5. Do you think God could be beyond our concept of what is fair and unfair? How?

¹³No one undergoing a trial should say, "I am being tempted by God." For God is not tempted by evil, and He Himself doesn't tempt anyone. ¹⁴But each person is tempted when he is drawn away and enticed by his own evil desires. ¹⁵Then after desire has conceived, it gives birth to sin, and when sin is fully grown, it gives birth to death.   JAMES 1:13-15

6.   According to the verses taken from James above, what circumstances do you think make forgiveness necessary?

"Out, damned spot! Out, I say!" In the fifth act of William Shakespeare's *Macbeth*, Lady Macbeth's treacherous murder of King Duncan takes its toll and she begins obsessively washing her hands to alleviate her guilty conscience only to find herself unable to completely remove the stains of her actions.

1.   In what ways are we like Lady Macbeth, wringing our hands in an effort to remove stains that are not visible in the physical world?

2.   When do you feel most hopeless and in greatest need of forgiveness?

As Macbeth was obsessively trying to do something to take off the invisible stain, we also may develop routines, or formulas, if done as prescribed we think will eliminate the guilt from our lives. Like Macbeth, however, the stain will remain on our hearts.

– DANIEL –

I know I have many times tried to cover my mistakes with good deeds rather that just confess. To tell a joke to lighten the mood. To lie low until the storm of emotions dies down. Anything to avoid that most painful of questions, "will you forgive me?" It's such vulnerable state, waiting. We talk all the time about how forgiving ourselves is the hardest step. When I say I can't forgive myself, I'm really rejecting God's forgiveness, keeping him at arm's length.

– MARY ANN –

"If we claim to be without sin, we deceive ourselves and the truth is not in us. If we confess our sins, he is faithful and just and will forgive us our sins and purify us from all unrighteousness. If we claim we have not sinned, we make him out to be a liar."   1 JOHN 1:8-10A (NIV)

---

3.   **We are often tempted to try to keep up the façade of perfectionism, but what does John say is the disastrous result of that game?**

---

¹Job answered ... ²⁴Why do you stay hidden and silent? Why treat me like I'm your enemy? ²⁵Why kick me around like an old tin can? Why beat a dead horse? ²⁶You compile a long list of mean things about me, even hold me accountable for the sins of my youth. ²⁷You hobble me so I can't move about. You watch every move I make, and brand me as a dangerous character.   JOB 13:1,24-27 (MSG)

After the LORD had finished speaking to Job, He said to Eliphaz the Temanite: "I am angry with you and your two friends, for you have not spoken the truth about Me, as My servant Job has..."   JOB 42:7

"Your name will no longer be Jacob," He said. "It will be Israel because you have struggled with God and with men and have prevailed."   GENESIS 32:28

---

4. Read the passages from Job given above. What do you think these verses say about the relationship between honesty and forgiveness?

5. Read Genesis 32:28. What characteristic of Jacob does Scripture seem to honor?

Behold, You desire truth in the innermost being, And in the hidden part You will make me know wisdom.   PSALM 51:6 (NASB)

---

6. Psalm 51:6 reveals that God desires truth—not just truth, but truth in the innermost, or "inmost," being—truth in the deepest places. As you consider the deep magic that is God's forgiveness, how do you think you can be more honest with Him?

Can you really forgive someone just halfway? To me, that's not true forgiveness. I think it's an all or nothing deal. How would you feel if God or others forgave you just halfway. I don't think it works like that.

– BARRY –

This characteristic honored seems more than just a "relationship" with God. It has to do with Jacob's candid behavior with God. Beyond honesty, but actually struggling with God! Jacob's standing with God didn't seem to have much to do with one little recited prayer.

– DANIEL –

The fact is that those who proclaim Jesus have claimed the forgiveness that God has extended. Many times, however, we opt for a partial credit in this aspect of our spiritual journey because we hold something back—maybe a relationship or a particular emotion. God is on record as revealing Himself to be a jealous God, but His jealousy is for our hearts. To experience the magic and mystery of forgiveness at its purest most intense level, we must be willing to open our hearts even in the darkest corners.

The following CANVAS Treatment is a separate group experience. We recommend either getting together in smaller, more intimate groups or the entire group. This Bridge activity is included as a continuation of your journey into the mystery of forgiveness.

I was never good at small talk, but I'm getting better. Not everyone who asks, "How are you?" really wants to know how you are. What they want is for you to be fine, so they can go ahead and talk about the weather, or the game, or ask a favor or tell you a joke. To listen to someone confess their imperfections means that for a moment, we might have to examine our own.

– MARY ANN –

THE BRIDGE

An Unfinished Life (2005)
>*Directed by Lasse Hallstrom*
>*Writing credits: Mark Spragg and Virginia Korus Spragg*
>*Starring: Robert Redford, Jennifer Lopez, Morgan Freeman, Josh Lucas*
>*MPAA: Rated PG-13 for some violence including domestic abuse and language*
>*Runtime: 107 minutes*

Take a night to get together as a group to watch *An Unfinished Life* with Robert Redford, Morgan Freeman, and Jennifer Lopez—a great show for a summer night or cozy winter evening. Grill some hamburgers or order pizza and slip into the frontier world where everything that happens happens bigger.

As you settle into the story we ask you to pay close attention to the bear, Mitch's bear, and how it plays so largely in the psyche of the movie itself. Each character, in some form or fashion, is affected by the bear. But it is Mitch that apparently holds the key.

As a group—or among yourselves—engage these questions:

In what way is Mitch released by the bear?
In what way is the bear released by Mitch and why do you think it matters?

**Describe Mitch's wounds. Are they entirely physical,
or are there deep wounds within his internal world?**

What deep magic takes place during his final confrontation with the bear?

QUESTIONS TO TAKE TO YOUR HEART

Where are those places deep within me most in
need of the deep magic of God's forgiveness?

In what ways do my emotions express the
need for the mystery of forgiveness?

QUESTIONS TO TAKE TO GOD

In what ways have I been less than honest with you, God?

THE MYSTERY OF FREEDOM

FRAME

There is a song produced on the 1979 record *The Wall* in which the artist reflects, "When I was a child I caught a fleeting glimpse out of the corner of my eye. I turned to look but it was gone. I cannot put my finger on it now." Most of us have caught a sudden scent hanging in the air that takes us to another place, but only for a moment. Or maybe you've had a sudden thought, lightning fast, and it's gone so fast you don't even know what it was —only feeling the emotional extremes left behind. The mystery of freedom works in much the same way. We only catch it in glimpses, maybe out of the corner of our eye or in the deepest places in our heart or maybe in an invisible and serendipitous cloud of Chanel No. 5.

Spiritually we catch inspired glimpses of "what once was" and "what will be again." But then the uber-reality of our broken world and battered lives invades our daydream and we wake up, somewhat startled, feeling much less than free. We find ourselves in the same realization as the writer of Romans: "Something has gone wrong deep within me and gets the better of me every time" (Romans 7:20, MSG).

CANVAS

1 HAVE YOU FOUND YOURSELF CATCHING GLIMPSES OF JOY IN THE REMOTE PLACES OF YOUR HEART? DESCRIBE THE FEELING. WHY DO YOU THINK WE CATCH THESE MOMENTS IN GLIMPSES?

2 WHAT STANDS BETWEEN YOU AND ABSOLUTE FREEDOM? IF ANY OBSTACLES WERE REMOVED, HOW WOULD YOUR LIFE BE IMPACTED?

The first year of college is a special time. When my parents left me at my dorm the first thought that came to my mind was, "now what?" I remember learning about the area where my college was located, in Louisville, KY. All of the coffee shops, parks, and restaurants were there for me to enjoy as I wanted to. I began to feel the freedom that comes with leaving home. There is something exciting about being able to do what you want, when you want. Yet there is something deceptive about it as well.

While we look at our lives, and the decisions we make, we perceive that we are free. Unfortunately, what we don't realize is that we have wrapped ourselves in chains and become slaves to these desires that we expect to fill us up. The appearance of freedom disappears as we continually return to our passions, even driven by them.

I used to think I was free earlier in life, yet realized that the things I thought would fill me began to control me. I was not free, nor had I ever been. It's only when you actually surrender your life that you become free.

— *DANIEL* —

PRIME

<<<Show Video 2/6, Unpacked>>>

The question Pete poses at the beginning of the video is a provocative question. What if you could live a day backwards? We like to imagine that if we were armed with a full understanding of the consequences of our actions we would make the right choice every time. But let's face it, the vast majority of the time we know what we should do, but we still don't do it.

For I do not do the good that I want to do, but I practice the evil that I do not want to do.　　　　　ROMANS 7:19

1.　Read Romans 7:19 above. Why do you think we live lives that are "less than free"?

2.　Pete notes that, statistically, there is little difference between believers who claim freedom and non-believers regarding issues such as divorce, depression, addictions, and substance abuse. Why do you think that is true?

3.　Do you share Pete's sentiment that despite the reminder in Romans, some days we feel quite confident that sin is alive and well within us? Describe that feeling. How do you think it is related to your freedom?

4. Why do you think freedom is only glimpsed between the moments of doing and not doing mentioned in Romans 7?

5. In the video "Unpacked," Pete says, "Part of the problem is that we want to trust Christ for our forgiveness, but we don't want to trust Him for our freedom." How do you think "freedom" and "forgiveness" are related?

The problem is that although believers have a new heart, the imprint of sin remains. There is an element of freedom that can be ours here, during this lifetime, and in this physical world. The taint of the fall, however, prevents this from being the outright reality. We are not only bound by physical limitations, but also disease and pain and our own stories. But there is a coming freedom. The mystery of freedom is a spiritual kaleidescope that moves in and out of colorful focus.

SKETCH

While we tend to define ourselves by the things we do, God instead knows us through our essence. The Latin word for heart is where we get our word "core." Scripture tells us that God looks at the heart of a person, our center. Although "heart" in some ways defies definition, it is perhaps best defined by saying that the heart is what most people mean when they use the word "me."

I chose you before I formed you in the womb; I set you apart before you were born. I appointed you a prophet to the nations.

JEREMIAH 1:5

"I will put my law in their minds and write it on their hearts. I will be their God, and they will be my people." *JEREMIAH 31:33 (NIV)*

I think forgiveness blazes the trail or paves the way for freedom. It's a means to an end. The other question, then, is "What's the freedom for?"

– BARRY –

We love familiarity. We like to know exactly what to expect. I used to work for a television station and if a show changed time slots or was interrupted by breaking news, there were bound to be tons of angry viewers calling to express discontent over the disruption. Maybe we're no different. Maybe we're a little uncomfortable blazing a path into the unfamiliar territory that comes with true freedom. Maybe we'd rather just hang on to life as we already know it.

– AUDRA –

1. Read Jeremiah 1:5. What does "set you apart" mean to you?

2. According to Jeremiah 31:33, the law is written on our hearts. How do you think we can be "free" when the law is imprinted at our most intimate places?

3. Look again at Romans 7:19. If the Law is written on our hearts and on our minds, then why do you think we don't do what we want all the time, but instead practice the evil mentioned in the passage?

> [31]*To the Jews who had believed him, Jesus said, "If you hold to my teaching, you are really my disciples.* [32]*Then you will know the truth, and the truth will set you free. ..."*   JOHN 8:31-32 (NIV)

> *"You have your heads in your Bibles constantly because you think you'll find eternal life there. But you miss the forest for the trees. These Scriptures are all about me! And here I am, standing right before you, and you aren't willing to receive from me the life you say you want.*   JOHN 5:39-40 (MSG)

---

4. According to John 8 above, where is freedom found?

5. In John 5:39-40 Jesus tells His audience that they are not willing to accept the life they say they want. What life do you think He is referring to? Why do you think these people will not accept a life of freedom?

6. How do you think freedom could be written into the DNA of a believer, yet the believer not be truly free?

Freedom comes in many forms. You are free to buy groceries and you are free to break the law. You are free within the laws of the government and you are free to come and go as you please. And there are deeper versions of freedom that are far less tangible. These freedoms are not as visible to us in the physical world and the lack of this sort of freedom is easily disguised, mysterious in nature, and can be elusive. Of course, the absence of freedom can be equally hidden.

STRETCH

Think back to Pete's comments about choice and the ability to live life in reverse. The absence of freedom can usually be traced back to our own decisions. So where is God during these times? Simply put, God not only allows us to make our own decisions, He also honors our choices.

1. Do you believe a person who believes "wholeheartedly" in Christ can still choose the wrong path? Why or why not?

_____

Christ has liberated us into freedom. Therefore stand firm and don't submit again to a yoke of slavery.   GALATIANS 5:1

_____

2. Read Galatians 5:1. Why did Jesus come into our world?

We are never finished becoming and fulfilling the plans God has for us. We will sin. I know I have believed wholeheartedly but that has not exempted me from the unfortunate detour or two. I think the more we imprint memories along the journey, the more we have to draw on when we are searching to get back on the right path.

– MARY ANN –

I accepted Jesus as my Savior when I was in high school. "What a relief," I thought. "This is just the best news a person could ever have." My mistake was thinking that something had ended; that life after that would be something real close to a Disney movie. The truth is, what I accepted was an invitation into something grand—something significant. Far from over, my heart would be under attack forever, the taint of the Fall remaining, and my life became suddenly more meaningful. The difference was the new weapons that I had in my transformation— weapons to fight bondage and injustice. Jesus is the difference maker.

– BRIAN –

For our battle is not against flesh and blood, but against the rulers, against the authorities, against the world powers of this darkness, against the spiritual forces of evil in the heavens. EPHESIANS 6:12

---

3. Do you think the fight for our freedom is done, over? If not, then what remains?

4. How do you think we are supposed to carry this fight for our freedom? Where is the battleground of this fight? Who are the players? What is at stake?

5. How do you think this battle is played out in the unseen world—the spiritual realm?

We have a crucial role to play in the fight for our own freedom. The battle is fought both here in the physical world but also in the unseen world against the powers of darkness and the spiritual forces of evil. Each of us is invited into this larger story where the stakes are high, the ammunition is real, and things are not always as they seem.

GLOSS

Most everyone can relate to the sense of calm inherent in the glassy surface of a lake or pond. If you've ever picked up a stone and thrown it into the deep you can recall the disturbance and the resulting ripples that move away from the center. The disturbance across the surface is indicative of what is unseen as the rock sinks deeper and deeper into the depths of a mysterious and unseen world.

1. **How do you think our lives are similar to the stone illustration above?**

Surely you desire truth in the inner parts; you teach me wisdom in the inmost place.   PSALM 51:6 (NIV)

2. **Psalm 51:6 stresses the importance of being honest in the "inner parts." What specifically do you think this passage is asking you to consider?**

3. **How do you think Psalm 51:6 applies to the mystery of freedom?**

Before I realized how important it was to seek out wise counsel, I went to see a counselor who turned out to be a little on the "New Agey" side. She talked a lot about positive energy and how we could get back in touch with ours, thus creating a "safe space" for communication with other people. Little did she realize that the hurt and issues I was dealing with needed a lot more than a positive patch! They were wounds that only God could fully treat and strongholds from which only He could set me free.

– AUDRA –

They dress the wound of my people as though it were not serious. 'Peace, peace,' they say, when there is no peace.   _JEREMIAH 6:14 (NIV)_

4. According to Jeremiah 6:14 (previous page), what angers God about the way the leaders of Jeremiah's day treated His people? Why?

5. Do you think Jeremiah 6:14 refers to the visible wounds, or to wounds in deeper places? Where do you think these wounds may have been inflicted in your own story?

The shameful secrets I keep in my heart are, too many times, on the tip of my tongue. They are perched and in position to be released from my innermost being. But they are, too many times, kept hush-hush—imprisoned within myself, and reciprocating their condition back to me.

– BARRY –

6. What are your deepest wounds and how have they been treated superficially?

The mystery of freedom comes down to this. We can live in the physical world as free people, doing what we please and acting as if we're free from our compulsions, our vows, and our wounds. External behavior modification is commensurate with freedom in this paradigm. That is certainly an option. Or we can choose to visit the deepest places that lie beyond the superficial repair jobs that we've built much of our reality upon. It's the difference between a freedom we see and act or a freedom we can breathe deep into who we are.

> *¹The Spirit of the Lord God is on Me, because the Lord has anointed Me to bring good news to the poor. He has sent Me to heal the brokenhearted, to proclaim liberty to the captives, and freedom to the prisoners; ²to proclaim the year of the Lord's favor, and the day of our God's vengeance; to comfort all who mourn, ... ³to give them a crown of beauty instead of ashes ... splendid clothes instead of despair. And they will be called righteous trees, planted by the Lord, to glorify Him.* ISAIAH 61:1-3

7. Read the passage from Isaiah given on the previous page. What wounds remain deep within your inner parts? What questions stand in the way of greater freedom?

The Layers Experience that follows is an individual exercise designed to be completed as a continuation of this conversation. This Bridge uses several passages from the Bible and specific questions. These Layers are designed to help you engage the Spirit to uncover the path to freedom.

CANVAS LAYERS EXPERIENCE

This journaling experience is a way to hear what God is revealing to you as you're transformed with ever-increasing glory. Respond to the Scripture and the following question in each of the next five instances. Once everyone has had an opportunity to prayerfully journal what God has revealed, schedule a time to get together to share what you've learned.

1: Flirting with Freedom

39You pore over the Scriptures because you think you have eternal life in them, yet they testify about Me. 40And you are not willing to come to Me that you may have life.   JOHN 5:39-40

Have you ever planned out a treasure hunt for someone close to you—maybe your sweetheart or spouse? You know, the cute little flirtatious clues you leave in different places, each one taking them from one clue to the next. You carefully and thoughtfully plan the details—placing love notes here and there. You make sure they don't get lost. You can't wait for them to reach the end. You hope they don't get sidetracked because a token of your heart's affection awaits their discovery.

God has been dropping clues around us since the beginning of time. Except these clues are more like bright neon signs. They are so obvious to see. From picturesque creation to personal conscience... from His written Word to eye-witnesses... from Jesus alive to dead, and back alive again... God brings us down His path. He wants us to discover something. In fact, our journey tells the story and reveals the evidence of God's love for us. And like our little trail of love notes we leave for our lovers, God's love points us to an unimaginable treasure: Himself. And the mission? Life. One of which can be described as a journey to finding true freedom.

In what way has your experience with Jesus put you on the path to freedom? Have you been distracted off the journey because of what you think you need to find? Have you been disappointed along the way?

"Instead, this is the covenant I will make with the house of Israel after those days"—the LORD's declaration. "I will place My law within them and write it on their hearts. I will be their God, and they will be My people.   ***JEREMIAH 31:33***

When was the last time you used the word "covenant" with your boss, or friend, or your local gas attendant? Probably never. The reason is because covenant is a word used to describe a strong and binding love-relationship. It goes beyond the idea of signing a contract or "shaking on it." It is the way God speaks His deepest love language to us.

Just think about what God promises in His Scripture. He promises to take what is on the outside [which affects our volition], and position it on the inside [which affects our attention and affection]. It is moving the letter of the law—which could never be perfectly followed, and transforming it into the spirit of the law—which allows us to follow in spite of imperfection. The difference is like night and day. It is the difference between attempting to keep up with a harsh taskmaster and being eternally inspired to follow the Beautiful One.

The result of this God-promise is a chance at freedom. Freedom to explore a genuine relationship with God. Freedom to be in the presence of the One who created us. Freedom to investigate all the goodness He has in store for us. Freedom to enjoy Him in spite of our messiness.

What is keeping you from exploring, investigating, and enjoying who God is to the fullest extent? What has God written on your heart?

---

*¹The Spirit of the Lord G*OD *is on Me, because the L*ORD *has anointed Me to bring good news to the poor. He has sent Me to heal the brokenhearted, to proclaim liberty to the captives, and freedom to the prisoners; ²to proclaim the year of the L*ORD*'s favor, and the day of our God's vengeance; to comfort all who mourn, ³to provide for those who mourn in Zion; to give them a crown of beauty instead of ashes, festive oil instead of mourning, and splendid clothes instead of despair. And they will be called righteous trees, planted by the L*ORD*, to glorify Him.*

ISAIAH 61:1-3

Isaiah 61:1-3 was written in a time when Israel needed to hear it the most. This passage meant something special to God's people in Isaiah's day because they were suffering, beaten down by their enemies, and feeling abandoned by God because of their own sin. Their hearts were broken. Just like Israel in Isaiah's time, we also have suffered the effects of our sin. They keep us bound and captive. Today, we need hope of a freedom that God can proclaim over us.

On the spiritual journey there is no enduring joy to be found in the good things of this life. In fact, the troubled heart may actually be an indication of emotional health in the realization that the fulfillment of ultimate desire must wait. Although our freedom comes incrementally throughout our lifetimes, the final and penultimate fulfillment of everything we long for must wait.

These verses presuppose our brokenness. In other words, we are not born free—as much as we may want to believe otherwise. The process of becoming free is a work that continues over the course of our lives as we allow the healing work of Jesus to speak into layer after layer after layer.

After reading this passage, what has to be true about what God thinks about you?

For our battle is not against flesh and blood, but against the rulers, against the authorities, against the world powers of this darkness, against the spiritual forces of evil in the heavens.   ***EPHESIANS 6:12***

Just before and right after this verse, Paul instructs the Christ-followers at Ephesus to "put on the full armor of God." Two times he gives this command. Why? Because our enemy is constantly thinking, and scheming, and strategizing new ways to steal our freedom in Christ. We cannot see the spiritual forces that wage war against us, so the mystery of our freedom becomes even more mysterious when it is lost or stolen.

Even though our freedom is granted to us, we must learn how to fight the enemy to preserve it. The dilemma is we cannot see our enemy, and the weapons we have feel awkward because we haven't had much practice using them. Nevertheless, without this warrior mind set and God's armor close by, we will be defeated by the schemes of the enemy. He has been at it way too long.

Can you point back to a time when you felt like the enemy stole your freedom away from you? What can you learn from that experience? To what degree would you be willing to wage war against the enemy to experience God's freedom once again? What do you think this war looks and feels like?

---

[31]So Jesus said to the Jews who had believed Him, "If you continue in My word, you really are My disciples. [32]You will know the truth, and the truth will set you free."

JOHN 8:31-32

What do you think Jesus would say to people who have heard His teaching, but still question His authority? What would He say to those who have seen Him raise people from the dead, but then spread it as a rumor? What about those who witnessed and tasted Jesus' goodness, then later complained it wasn't good enough? What do you think Jesus would say?

It looks like it has already been said. These are the people to whom Jesus is speaking in John 8:31-32. Essentially, this passage records Jesus' response to those who either followed Christ at a distance, or believed Him with half their heart. Jesus' teaching paves the way for truth. And truth blazes a trail for freedom. The bottom line is this: if you hang in there and follow His teaching, it will lead you to the truth, and that truth will set you free. The choice is yours to make.

Are there any difficult lessons that you are hesitant to learn or explore? Imagine God's story as one road, and your story as another. Have they crossed paths? Has the story of God's truth intersected with your desire to be free?

THE MYSTERY OF TRANSFORMATION

FRAME

The mystery of transformation only begins to address the wonderful and fantastic metamorphosis from what was old to what is new; what has gone away and what is to come. Is this an anatomical change during which our physical composition actually changes? Is this transformation visible to those around us, or does this only take place deep within? Or when we talk about our spiritual transformation are we simply talking about the decision to be better, to stop doing some things and start doing some other things?

The answer is yes. It's all of these things. The mystery of transformation is so out of control. It expands to include what has been lost and what may be recovered. The mystery of transformation harkens back to the Garden of Eden but also points to a coming day. It takes place deep within but is also manifested externally. It is complete and thorough, but also—at least in the world we currently occupy—somewhat limited. In this Canvas setting we're going to tell a story about the new heart of a believer.

1 WHAT IS ONE AREA OF YOUR LIFE WHERE YOU FEEL AN ONGOING STRUGGLE LETTING THE OLD GO AWAY, AND THE NEW HEART THRIVE?

2 MANY OF US ARE FAMILIAR WITH THE TERM "ORIGINAL SIN," BUT HOW WOULD YOU RESPOND TO THE TERM "ORIGINAL GLORY"?

CANVAS

Growing up my life was baseball. I'm quite confident that thousands of hours of my life were spent at the ballpark. I learned a lot of life lessons on the ball field. Probably the biggest is a lesson that Coach Mike taught me when I was around 10 years old. For a variety of reasons I was not having a good season. I wasn't hitting the ball and to make matters worse I was not doing a real good job at catching it either. In case you are not aware hitting and catching are the two primary things you need to do if you want to add value to the team.

For whatever reason, Coach Mike took an interest in me. He believed in me when there was really no good reason to do so. He was constantly affirming me. Constantly reminding me that I had what it takes to be a good ball player. His words of affirmation and the value that he breathed in to me made a big difference in my skill level. I watched my skill level transform over the course of a summer. Coach helped me see myself not for the player I was, but for the player I could become. He helped me move from what "was" to what "could be."

Isn't that exactly what God has done throughout all of history and still does today? He renamed Abram to Abraham. He called Simon to the new name of Peter. He is in the name changing business. He sees not who we are today but who He created us to be when He thought us into existence.

— PETE —

PRIME

‹‹‹Show Video 3/6, More›››

Ten pounds overweight with a color job gone terribly wrong during my last salon visit. That's how I see myself right now. On a good day, we can add creative, adventurous, and an excellent cook. I seriously hope God is seeing something else in there that I'm not, and that he will reveal it to me. Soon.

– AUDRA –

While most of our culture gets all warm and fuzzy when we talk about achieving our "inner potential," those of us who are honest with ourselves take a look inside and aren't always as positive about what we find there. It can be difficult for us to fully accept that as "new creations," "old things have passed away" and "new things have come."[1]

1. The video talks about a parent's desire for their children to see themselves as the parent sees them. How do you think God sees you?

2. How do you see yourself? How does that compare with how God sees you?

There was a time when I trusted most folks unless they gave me a reason not to. My naiveté hit me square in the eye at age 38 (when I should have known better.) Someone betrayed me and sadly... many innocents have felt the aftermath. Not only do I distrust the one who betrayed but, I am suspicious of others as well. Not fair, I know.

– MARY ANN –

3. Pete infers in the video that a major reason we don't exercise our God-given and Christ-restored potential is that we have major trust issues. Do you see the correlation between the two? In what ways?

4. When someone breaks your trust, what is your typical response?

So from now on we regard no one from a worldly point of view. ... Therefore, if anyone is in Christ, he is a new creation; the old has gone, the new has come! All this is from God, who reconciled us to himself through Christ and gave us the ministry of reconciliation.

2 CORINTHIANS 5:16-18 (NIV)

---

[1] *2 CORINTHIANS 5:17*

5. The world is constantly telling us that we are less, while 2 Corinthians 5:16-18 reminds us here that we are becoming more, with a new start in Christ. In what ways does the world attempt to distort and warp our view of ourselves?

6. Keeping the metaphor of a good Father who sees so much more in us than we see in ourselves, share something positive that you see about the God-given potential in the person seated on your right.

Most of us grapple with the hope of real and lasting transformation much like the initial reluctance of the boy approaching the bike. We want to experience something new and exciting, but we have all kinds of fears. We doubt ourselves. We know the journey ahead involves practice and probably more than a little pain. Ultimately, it is the encouragement of a patient and trustworthy dad that enables the boy to take a risk. And it is the voice of our patient and trustworthy heavenly Father that gives us the courage to be alive and risk new adventures, because in the end, He knows us better than we know ourselves.

SKETCH

When we make mistakes and fall short, we can justify it in a million ways: "I wasn't ready." "It's been a hard day." "I was misinformed." The list and the self-promises go on and on. But what if we're just fooling ourselves? Scripture brings us back to reality by confronting the illusion that we can fix ourselves by just doing it all better or trying harder. There is another aspect to this mystery.

The world will always view people based on external things. What kind of wardrobe do you have? What size house do you live in? How educated are you? We are judged by standards that are visible to us. When God looks at us none of those things matter. He sees how we are changing on the inside, not whether or not our lives are upgrading on the outside.

– DANIEL –

Now if I do what I do not want, I am no longer the one doing it, but it is the sin that lives in me.   **ROMANS 7:20**

1. Read Romans 7:20. When we first come to Christ, many people are under the false assumption that all their sinful desires will simply disappear once they accept Christ. Why do you think this is not the case?

2. Do you think acknowledging sin's signature on our lives means refusing responsibility for sin? If not, then what do you think this means?

I can't tell you how many times I've asked God to take me to a deeper level, to teach me more about patience, courage, or whatever and then, because I am not as much of a risk taker as I like to think, I add, "And please, don't make the lessons too painful."

– AUDRA –

---

[21]So I find this law at work: When I want to do good, evil is right there with me. [22]For in my inner being I delight in God's law; [23]but I see another law at work in the members of my body, waging war against the law of my mind and making me a prisoner of the law of sin at work within my members.   *ROMANS 7:21-23 (NIV)*

---

3. How do you think the "inner being" and the other law "at work" compare as they are described in Romans 7:21-23 above?

4. How does this coincide with the mysterious fact that you are, at the same time, a new creation that is righteous in the eyes of God?

3Jesus replied, "I assure you: Unless someone is born again, he cannot see the kingdom of God." 4"But how can anyone be born when he is old?" Nicodemus asked Him. "Can he enter his mother's womb a second time and be born?" 5Jesus answered, "I assure you: Unless someone is born of water and the Spirit, he cannot enter the kingdom of God. 6Whatever is born of the flesh is flesh, and whatever is born of the Spirit is spirit. 7Do not be amazed that I told you that you must be born again. 8The wind blows where it pleases, and you hear its sound, but you don't know where it comes from or where it is going. So it is with everyone born of the Spirit."   JOHN 3:3-8

5. Jesus describes a strange process in the verses above. Where do you think this transformation takes place within a believer?

6. How would you define "heart"?

I guess I'm going to have to get used to living in the contradiction. If Jesus can be man and God at the same time, then I guess I can be declared righteous and struggle with sin simultaneously.

– BARRY –

The mystery of transformation takes place in the heart. This is not the organ that sends our blood with its valuable cargo on its way nor is it the cartoon that we see most often around Valentine's Day. "Core" might come closest, but it still reduces this aspect of who we are to a specific place—and we are all much more than that. We cannot escape the fact that Jesus is referring to a total transformation; totally new.

STRETCH

"I will give you a new heart and put a new spirit in you; I will remove your heart of stone and give you a heart of flesh. I will place My Spirit within you and cause you to follow My statutes and carefully observe My ordinances."
EZEKIEL 36:26-27

To be honored, we don't use that word often to describe our daily living. Honors, those are for career benchmarks, personal achievements, anniversaries, milestone birthdays...but God does every day of our lives! It's difficult for me to balance the humility that Jesus taught with the delight of being "fearfully and wonderfully made." To be honored means we are treated as special, and given more than what is expected. I need more of that... to be delighted with the glory and honor God has bestowed on me.

– MARY ANN –

1. Ezekiel 36 describes the old heart as being like stone and the new heart as being made of flesh. What do you think these two words mean? What words would you use to describe the old heart and the new heart?

So God created man in His own image; He created him in the image of God; He created them male and female. *GENESIS 1:27*

⁴what is man that You remember him, the son of man that You look after him? ⁵You made him a little less than God and crowned him with glory and honor. *PSALM 8:4-5*

2. Read Genesis 1:27. What do you think is truest about you?

3. What do you think Genesis 1:27 and Psalm 8:4-5 reveal about what you were created to be?

⁶The woman saw that the tree was good for food and delightful to look at, and that it was desirable for obtaining wisdom. So she took some of its fruit and ate it; she also gave some to her husband, who was with her, and he ate it. ⁷Then the eyes of both of them were opened, and they knew they were naked.   GENESIS 3:6-7

4.   Describe what was lost in the act reported in Genesis 3 above.

5.   What do you think the spiritual transformation Jesus describes in John 3 (see page 45) recovers from our original state?

We all, with unveiled faces, are reflecting the glory of the Lord and are being transformed into the same image from glory to glory ... "
2 CORINTHIANS 3:18

6.   Take a look at 2 Corinthians 3:18. Do you think this transformation could be a total recovery of what we lost in the garden of Eden? Why or why not? How is this difficult to comprehend?

On one hand this conversion is very difficult to comprehend while on the other it couldn't be more simple. It's a strange and mysterious duplicity that confronts us. How can we fall in accordance with Genesis 3 only to be transformed with the new heart God promises... yet Romans 7 tells us that we still don't always do what our new heart wants to do. Not only do we not do what we ought, but when we don't it's not really us that's making the decision—not the real you (7:20); not what's truest about the transformed and re-born you.

We have been fighting to get back into the garden since we were tossed out. From the pursuit of leisure to the promise of epidurals, we've been trying to assuage the painful results of missing the mark.

– BARRY –

We can't "unknow" what Adam and Eve learned for us in the Garden. Their sin changed the relationship completely. I guess I look at that sin and think we have the potential to know God better than we would if it had never happened. How would we ever know the concept of forgiveness, had they never first disobeyed.

– MARY ANN –

GLOSS

In the movie *Gladiator* (2000), the hero, Maximus, lives the path from general to slave to gladiator to the man who saved a nation. At one point a member of his band, Juba, tells him, "You have a great name. [The enemy] must kill your name before he kills you." Juba's observation suggests that the name, the identity, the essence, is somehow different and separate—maybe even greater—than the man.

I have held on to expectations... to patterns of behavior that "didn't fit" simply because there was comfort in the familiar. With God's help, I can overhaul my heart... get rid of the things that are too tight... cast off the pieces that are shapeless and drab. Introduce color and pattern that I was never brave enough to try.

– MARY ANN –

1. How do you think the mystery of transformation can lead to a new identity that is great beyond who you are?

> *[2]For this reason God also highly exalted Him and gave Him the name that is above every name, [10]so that at the name of Jesus every knee should bow ... [11]and every tongue should confess that Jesus Christ is Lord.*
> PHILIPPIANS 2:9-11

2. What does Philippians 2:9-11 reveal about the name of Jesus as it relates to our own transformation? In what way(s) is His name separate from His being, if any?

> *Anyone who has an ear should listen to what the Spirit says ... I will give the victor ... a white stone, and on the stone a new name is inscribed that no one knows except the one who receives it.*
> REVELATION 2:17

3. According to Revelation 2:17, with our new heart each of us also receives a name from God that only the two of us will know. How do you think God determines what this name is?

4. How do you think this is a part of the mystery of transformation?

5. Take another look at 2 Corinthians 3:18. To what do you think this process of transformation, of "glory to glory," ultimately points?

Do not conform any longer to the pattern of this world, but be transformed ...   **ROMANS 12:2 (NIV)**

Later on in *Gladiator* both Maximus and Juba express their belief that there is a time coming when they both will be fully restored to a prior and unspoiled condition—but not yet.

6. How do you think God will reveal your new name to you? When?

The Bridge experience that follows includes both individual and group aspects. It begins with layered journal experiences followed by a separate group get-together.

I've never really thought about it before, but I think this is speaking of an intimate relationship between God and me. You know, when two lovers have those "secret nicknames" for each other. Or, when two close friends have that "secret hand shake."

– BARRY –

CANVAS LAYERS EXPERIENCE

This journaling experience is a way to hear what God is revealing to you as you're transformed with ever-increasing glory. Respond to the Scripture and the following question in each of the next three instances. Once everyone has had an opportunity to prayerfully journal what God has revealed, schedule a time to get together to share what you've learned.

Transformation Storyboard 1:

The Lord your God is among you, a warrior who saves. He will rejoice over you with gladness ... He will delight in you with shouts of joy.   *ZEPHANIAH 3:17*

13For it was You who created my inward parts; You knit me together in my mother's womb. 14I will praise You, because I have been remarkably and wonderfully made. Your works are wonderful, and I know this very well.   *PSALM 139:13-14*

Use the space below to respond to this question to take *to God*:

God, what do you enjoy most about me?

Transformation Storyboard 2:

We all, with unveiled faces, are reflecting the glory of the Lord and are being transformed into the same image from glory to glory ..."   *2 CORINTHIANS 3:18*

Use the space below to respond to this question to take *to your heart*:

When do I feel most alive?
What makes me feel most alive?

One of those listening was a woman named Lydia ... who was a worshiper of God.
The Lord opened her heart to respond ..." ACTS 16:14 (NIV)

Use the space below to respond to this question to take *to God*:

How do you want to continue transforming my heart, Lord?

Transformation Storyboard 3:

Do not conform any longer to the pattern of this world, but be transformed ...
ROMANS 12:2 (NIV)

Anyone who has an ear should listen to what the Spirit says ... . I will give the victor
... a white stone, and on the stone a new name is inscribed that no one knows except
the one who receives it. *REVELATION 2:17*

Use the space below to respond to this question to take *to your heart*:

How is the mystery of spiritual transformation more than my name?
How does the mystery of transformation
have everything to do with my name?

Use the space below to respond to this question to *take to God*:

Lord, how can I experience more of You?
How can I begin to be the person You have created me to be?

A TAPESTRY OF TRANSFORMATION

Get together to share your storyboards with the group. Begin the time by answering this question: What surprised you the most? We've included a recipe for our world-famous salsa to enjoy during this time for sharing the story of transformation that God has begun to reveal to you.

World Famous Salsa

¼ tsp. garlic

4 med. tomatoes

½ med. onion, chopped

Cilantro

1 green pepper, chopped

½ lime

Tabasco

Salt

Pepper

¾ tsp. olive oil

Lemon juice, tbsp

THE MYSTERY OF THE HOLY SPIRIT

FRAME

Maybe the word "indwelling" isn't something that you hear all that often. "Indwelling." "Dwell" is present tense as in "right now, all the time." Make it "indwell" and it means "within you, right now, all the time." Add to that a voice and a divine knowledge and you've got somewhere close to the mystery of the Holy Spirit.

The Holy Spirit, referred to as the Holy Ghost for quite some time, most likely isn't an unfamiliar notion to you. After all, we're talking about the Third Person of the Trinity. But have you really stopped to consider the extremely supernatural aspects that make up this part of the faith? He is everywhere, all the time, and speaks to all of us about various things. Among all the voices in the world, the Holy Spirit is the most important, yet is most likely the quietest, the gentlest, and most nurturing. Also known as the Spirit of Truth, the Holy Spirit is the most personal presence in our lives—possibly more personal that your relationship with yourself.

1 WHAT THOUGHTS ARE GENERALLY CONJURED WHEN YOU HEAR THE WORD "SPIRIT"?

2 HOW ARE GHOSTS AND SPIRITS TYPICALLY PORTRAYED IN HOLLYWOOD? WHY DO YOU THINK THIS IS SO? HOW DO YOU THINK THIS HAS TAINTED OUR UNDERSTANDING OF THE HOLY SPIRIT?

CANVAS

There were two things in my parent's house that were never tolerated: lying and laziness. You did what you had to do, then you could do what you wanted to do. Personal responsibility and self – reliance was the family credo. While neither of my parents was extravagant with praise, when I did receive it, I know it was from loving hearts, where admiration and honor had been germinating. Though they modeled gratitude and giving, I was taught that most good things come from working smarter and harder. That life's successes and failures were about being able to adapt and make "good" choices. As a child, my prayers were about giving thanks and honoring God. But when it came to a tight spot, a trouble in my heart, I would tell myself that God was much too busy with "real" problems and if I just strengthened my resolve, I could reason out a solution soon enough. And in the mean time, I could spin it. Lying was easier than admitting that I was afraid, or that I might be in over my head. I loved the Lord, but I didn't want to be obliged. Ignorance or arrogance, a big helping of both.

For many years, I rarely thought about the availability of the Holy Spirit, right there with me, just waiting for an invitation to amaze me... To show me what I could be and do and feel with the power of Jesus living in me. One day, I had to confront some very painful truths. My life was going to change immensely, and I was one of the last to know. No way to spin it, to gloss it, no way to avoid the pain that was coming. It felt unfamiliar but so comforting, the wind that helped me up, ahead and towards healing. I knew that day, that I never wanted to be without the warm breath of God.

— MARY ANN —

PRIME

‹‹‹Show Video 4/6, White Out›››

According to a 2006 *USA Today®* article, the average person still spends about four and a half hours a day watching television. That translates into more than 1,600 hours a year, and over 12 uninterrupted years by the time we are 65, of someone else's agenda, someone else's message being pounded inside our heads. And that was before we added the age of cell phones, e-mail, blogs and Internet social networking to the list.

Growing up, my particular church was leery of people who spoke about the Holy Spirit. He was such a mystery, I think we were just afraid of the whole concept of living in the Spirit. The aversion was so great, the first message I heard about the Holy Spirit was when I was eighteen.

– BARRY –

1. In the video, Pete asks, "At the end of the day, what will be the prevailing message in your mind, and where did it come from?" Before your head hit the pillow last night, what were you thinking about?

2. Do you find it difficult to "turn off the noise"?

3. Using the metaphor of sailing in an enormous ocean full of crashing waves and undercurrents, how do you think you're supposed to hear just one voice?

4. Pete gives a very strong description of the Holy Spirit as our rudder in that ocean, a voice that is "oddly calm, mysteriously present, gentle and omniscient." Which of those phrases resonates with you, or what phrase would you add to describe the Holy Spirit?

5. Do you agree that we don't just stumble across this "voice of Truth," but that the Holy Spirit searches us out? How? By what means?

6. Do you think we hear this voice through physical means as with other voices, or by some other means—something beyond physical? If so, what?

SKETCH

The night prior to Jesus' death sentence was heavy with significance. Most likely the disciples could feel the weightiness of the moment. Jesus aptly began with encouragement—words the disciples would cling to in the emotional three days ahead.

"And I will ask the Father, and he will give you another Counselor to be with you forever — the Spirit of truth. ... You know him, for he lives with you and will be in you."   John 14:16-17 (NIV)

---

1. In the passage above Jesus tells the disciples about the Holy Spirit. What do you suppose Jesus meant when He said, "You know him"?

2. Where does the Holy Spirit reside? Talk about the mysteries that surface as you answer this question.

My first physical recognition of the Holy Spirit happened at a wedding. A tiny simple, country church with a baptismal pond out back. After the couple exchanged vows, a soloist began the first few bars of "Sweet, Sweet Spirit." You could hear folks humming along. It was so warm and comforting. I remember wanting to keep breathing really deeply.

– MARY ANN –

> [26]"But the Counselor, the Holy Spirit, whom the Father will send in my name, will teach you all things and will remind you of everything I have said to you. [27]... Do not let your hearts be troubled and do not be afraid."
>
> *JOHN 14:26-27 (NIV)*

3. Why do you think we need the Holy Spirit as our constant spiritual companion?

> The Spirit Himself testifies together with our spirit that we are God's children, and if children, also heirs — heirs of God and co-heirs with Christ — seeing that we suffer with Him so that we may also be glorified with Him.
>
> *ROMANS 8:16-17*

4. Look at the passage above. Does this mean that the Holy Spirit will always make life easy for a believer? Why or why not?

> God created man in His own image, in the image of God He created him; male and female He created them.
>
> *GENESIS 1:27 (NASB)*

> The LORD is a warrior, Yahweh is His name.
>
> *EXODUS 15:3*

5. Look at the two verses above. If God is the Father, then why do you think He sent the Spirit to us?

The Holy Spirit is the gentle, tender, compassionate, and nurturing side of God. The Holy Spirit is the nearest reflection of Eden that we have. Exodus 15:3 proclaims God as a warrior and certainly Scripture attests to this again and again. Perhaps God the Father embodies the strength of the Trinity while the Holy Spirit is the purest embodiment of Beauty. Or maybe these lines are unclear without clear delineations.

6.   In what ways do you think beauty is mysterious? How can these concepts be applied to the Holy Spirit?

STRETCH

Inherent in beauty is a profound depth that has the power to move us emotionally and inspire us to greater and greater heights. Beauty is vulnerable and delicate. Beauty at its purest has the lightest of touches yet wields the greatest power. Imagine a beauty that does not boast and that is not proud; not rude or self-seeking nor easily angered nor a keeper of wrongs.

Now the earth was formless and empty, darkness was over the surface of the deep, and the Spirit of God was hovering over the waters.   *GENESIS 1:2 (NIV)*

---

1.   Keeping in mind that Genesis isn't the beginning of the Larger Story, but only the beginning of the human story, and that "hovering" can also be interpreted as "brooding," what is the mood of the Spirit of God in the scene described in Genesis 1:2?

2.   What do you think Genesis 1:2 might reveal about the nature, or heart, of the Holy Spirit? In what ways do you think the Holy Spirit might be emotional?

As I've gotten older the whole concept of beauty has taken on entirely new levels. In fact, I'm not even sure how I would define it anymore. There are so many layers ... there is the physical aspect and there is the emotional aspect. Sometimes I'm moved by something and I don't even know why. All I know is that beauty at its purest lies beyond my own understanding and my heart is the only part of me that speaks the language well enough to allow me to catch glimpses.

– BRIAN –

3. What do you think knowing the Holy Spirit as the emotional seat of the Trinity reveals about the Spirit's depth?

For prophecy never had its origin in the will of man, but men spoke from God as they were carried along by the Holy Spirit.

2 PETER 1:21 (NIV)

In the same way the Spirit also helps our weakness; for we do not know how to pray as we should, but the Spirit Himself intercedes for us with groanings too deep for words. ROMANS 8:26 (NASB)

---

4. What effect does the word "groanings" have in the verse above? What does the phrase "too deep for words" reveal about how the Holy Spirit interacts with us?

5. What do you think these two verses tell us about our weaknesses and how well the Holy Spirit knows us? How do you think the Holy Spirit could know you better than you know yourself?

In Taize, a short verse is repeated in song ...again and again. These repetitive chants grow louder and then soften to barely a whisper. It is a powerful way to prepare our hearts for prayer. In my worship community, we sing 'sighs too deep for words." Groaning certainly implies more desperation. Privately we groan, publicly we sigh? Groan or sigh, we use both when we are exhausted. It's a sound we utter when we are spent, when we need to catch a Breath...

– MARY ANN –

GLOSS

In the movie *Stranger than Fiction*, Will Ferrell plays IRS agent Harold Crick. Harold has his mundane existence shattered by the prophetic voice of a female narrator who is describing his life as he's living it. Greatly troubled at first by this startling development, little does he know that over time, learning to listen to the voice will prompt him to truly live instead of just exist.

1. How is the Holy Spirit's role in our lives somewhat similar to that of the all-knowing narrator in *Stranger than Fiction*?

2. Think again about all the voices we heard in "More." How does it make you feel to know that the Holy Spirit is pursuing you through all the noise and haste?

3. In what ways does the Holy Spirit inspire us to live from the heart?

4. When the Holy Spirit thinks of you, what do you think He sees?

Sometimes an emotional switch will go off during times I would not normally show emotion. I've been around those who are in need, and suddenly I am overwhelmed with the desire to want to help them, even when there is nothing I can do for them physically. The Holy Spirit causes me to see things the way God sees them. This is why it is crucial to always be listening for Him.

– DANIEL –

28"I will pour out my Spirit on all people. Your sons and daughters will prophesy, your old men will dream dreams, your young men will see visions. ...30 I will show wonders in the heavens and on earth.

JOEL 2:28,30 (NIV)

---

5. In what ways does the Holy Spirit touch you in the deepest places of your being; places you didn't know existed; places no one else can touch?

The Stills Experience found on the next page is an individual Bridge exercise.

THE BRIDGE

Just as the Holy Spirit is complex with layers and layers of depth, you, too, are complex with many layers. The Third Person of the Trinity has chosen to indwell within your heart—the seat of your emotions. As the keeper of your story, your heart possesses the vastness of your internal world.

The Bridge this week asks you to respond on behalf of your internal world. The story that God is telling through you must be channeled through your heart as the Spirit of Truth reveals Himself to you. Use the space below to artistically represent your internal world. Remember, God doesn't love us despite our messes, but because of them. As we'll learn more about in the next setting, He's got it covered. So use pencils or pens or markers or whatever you can find. Ask the Holy Spirit to reveal to you what He sees deep inside you. As you engage this Stills experience you may want to listen to music from *Pursued by God: An Experience in Redemptive Worship*.

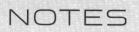

NOTES

NOTES

THE MYSTERY OF REDEMPTION

FRAME

Redemption is a word of incredible importance that turns up in the most unusual places in our world. We proudly redeem tickets from intense arcade games for some lame prize. Glass bottles have "redemption value" of a whopping 5 cents each in certain states. And we "graciously" comment on what we think must be someone's "only redeeming quality." The word finds its way into lots of songs and some very famous movies, but what does it really mean? And why is it a reoccurring theme in our world?

C.S. Lewis once said, "It is no good asking for a simple religion. After all, real things are not simple. They look simple, but they are not." Such is the case with redemption. It is one of the great themes of salvation—a mysterious process initiated and carried out by God, yet involving us as full participants in its drama. In this session we'll explore where this concept of redemption originates, why we need it, and how it will one day turn the world upside down—or more accurately, right side up again.

HOW DO YOU DEFINE "REDEMPTION"?

HOW HAVE YOU EXPERIENCED OR WITNESSED REDEMPTION?

12

CANVAS

I remember being a little confused growing up when people talked about "redemption." I don't recall what answers I got when I asked what it meant, but looking back my assumption is that my questions were answered with a cliché of some kind, or maybe by explaining what it means to "redeem" a coupon or get something for nothing. And for the longest time I would see "redemption" in its various associations. There are movies about redemption and stories of redemption ... but most of these definitions seemed bent on revenge and I thought surely something as profound and central as redemption couldn't be summed up in the simple act of getting back at somebody. But then I had a bizarre run of life that culminated with an experience I had with my father, a man I hadn't seen in about 10 years. As I drove away from that encounter I began to understand the power of God's redemption and what it meant. I recalled the passage in Romans that says "all things" will work for the good. As redemption took shape I realized that everything I see, hear, touch, feel, all the messes—everything—God promises to make good and right. I am overwhelmed by the sheer magnitude of this promise and, honestly, am mystified by it as well. Redemption is the ripple that moves across all of time and creation.

— BRIAN —

PRIME

‹‹‹Show Video 5/6, Not Yet›››

1. In the video Pete said, "There's just something magical and mysterious about redemption and restoration." What is it about the process that's magical to you?

2. Think about the fairy tales you've read or watched, whether from childhood or modern day. What hope is offered in these stories?

I flew through fairy tale books when I was a kid. I especially liked the story of Sleeping Beauty. There she was, snoozing away for decades while the castle grounds become overgrown with vines and weeds. How exciting when the prince's kiss broke the spell, awakened the princess, and restored order and beauty to the kingdom.

– AUDRA –

3. We learn in Romans 8:21 that creation itself longs to be "set free from its slavery" (NASB). What do you think keeps creation in chains, and how do you envision creation responding once it's been released?

4. Pete mentions that God began His work of redemption in the garden of Eden and has been working to redeem us ever since. How do you reconcile the fact that, as a Christian, you have already been redeemed by Christ's blood, yet God is still in a constant process of redeeming you?

5. Pete describes God as being on an eternal "rescue mission." What things in your life would you like to be rescued from right now?

SKETCH

To get our arms around this concept, we need to start at the beginning: God created, and it was good; Man fell, and it was bad—really bad—and its consequences far-reaching.

The whole world is under the control of the evil one.

1 JOHN 5:19 (NIV)

...until both creation and all the creatures are ready and can be released at the same moment into the glorious times ahead. Meanwhile, the joyful anticipation deepens.   *ROMANS 8:21 (MSG)*

---

1.   Look at 1 John 5:19 and Romans 8:21 above and describe our current state.

2.   What does this mean to us? How do you think the fall of man and our subsequent loss could even affect the trees, the mountains, the air—all of creation?

3.   If all is waiting, talk about what we're waiting for. Look again at Romans 8:21. What do you think it will look like when all is "released"?

Gosh, when I think of being redeemed it is easy to only think of being already redeemed by God. That insinuates that I don't need to be redeemed again, or any more than I already am. Thinking of the things that I need to be rescued from puts me back in perspective that although Jesus has rescued me from the eternal consequences, I am not totally rescued from the present day struggles.

– DANIEL –

He has made everything appropriate in its time. He has also put eternity in their hearts ...   *ECCLESIASTES 3:11*

---

4. In "Not Yet" Pete mentions several great stories. Why do you think these stories move us?

Why do epic dramas or adventures churn out record-breaking box office numbers and inspire multiple sequels? Because there's something in our spirit that inherently connects with another person's search for significance and makes us feel perfectly justified in shelling out $9.50 for a seat and $12.50 for popcorn and a coke so that we, too, can share in the story.

– AUDRA –

Honestly, when I try to wrap my brain around a concept like redemption, I need to get the duct tape out because I feel like my head is going to explode.

– BARRY –

5. Ecclesiastes 3:11 reveals that God has placed eternity into our hearts; that our hearts are wired to recognize ... something. What do you think this says about why we are moved by the great stories?

The mystery of redemption is the central drama of the Larger Story. When we pull back the curtain of reality and peer into the unseen world of principalities and powers we catch a glimpse of how the agents of God fight for us on the grandest stage. Our hearts are pre-wired to recognize the story of redemption when it is played out in our music or in our movies or in our lives. Our hearts are always cognizant of the Larger Story as it unfolds and manifests itself in our world.

STRETCH

When we begin to look at this much bigger picture, we're surprised to find ourselves in the middle of the drama of the ages. Just as Sam wondered aloud to Frodo, we catch ourselves wondering what sort of tale we have stumbled into. The Larger Story is very real and has all the elements —heroes, villains, a beauty to be rescued, advocates of both sides—that we recognize as part of the Epic.

---

[17]Your heart became proud because of your beauty; For the sake of your splendor you corrupted your wisdom. So I threw you down to the earth; I made a spectacle of you before kings. [18]You profaned your sanctuaries by the magnitude of your iniquities in your dishonest trade. So I sent out fire from within you, and it consumed you. I reduced you to ashes on the ground in the sight of everyone watching you. EZEKIEL 28:17-18

---

1. Ezekiel 28:17-18 describes the Villain in the Larger Story. Who are the players in the Larger Story? Who is the Villain?

[Christ came to] free those who were held in slavery all their lives by the fear of death.   HEBREWS 2:15

---

2. Who is the Hero-Redeemer of our stories? Describe His mission in some detail.

3. Where do you think this drama is unfolding? When?

4. What role do you think you have been called to play in God's plan of redemption?

5. What might prevent you from stepping into the role you have been created to play in the Larger Story?

The full- time role in the Larger Story is daunting. Can I still moonlight in other roles, too? What will I have to sacrifice to follow Him into this mission? What if this role consumes me? The possibility is exciting and a little scary.

– MARY ANN –

There are many distractions that this world can fly in my face. It is difficult at times to not "keep up with the Joneses" with all of the things that are available to us today. It always seems that an extra few hundred per month will be great so that we can have extra things around. This is distracting because it can take my time and focus away from the things of God.

– DANIEL –

And we know that God causes all things to work together for good to those who love God, to those who are called according to His purpose. *ROMANS 8:28 (NASB)*

6. What does Romans 8:28 tell us? What does this passage not promise?

GLOSS

I will repay you for the years that the swarming locust ate ... My people will never again be put to shame. *JOEL 2:25-26*

1. Read the passage from Joel above. What does God promise to do?

2. What is magical to you about the mystery of redemption?

3. In Joel 2:25 God promises to repay or "buy back" the years the swarming locusts have taken. What do the locusts represent for you in your life?

4. How do you think God is fighting for you right now?

The Treatment Experience for this setting has been included as a separate time of fellowship. Enjoy your time together and think through the questions we've included.

CANVAS TREATMENT EXPERIENCE

The Count of Monte Cristo (2002)
Directed by Kevin Reynolds
Writing credits: Alexandre Dumas, novel; Jay Wolpert (screenplay)
Starring: Jim Caviezel, Guy Pearce, Richard Harris
MPAA: Rated PG-13 for adventure violence/swordplay and some sensuality
Runtime: 131 minutes

Either as a group or in your own home, watch *The Count of Monte Cristo*.

1. When Edmond calls on God for help, his tormentor Dorleac says, "You ask God for help, and I'll stop the moment he shows up." How is this similar to the tactics the Villain in the Larger Story employs?

2. When Edmond denounces God, the priest responds with mercy, grace, and love. How do you think this is similar to how God responds to our messes?

3. How do you think God could be working behind the scenes in your life in a way similar to how Edmond's captivity was used?

4. In the Larger Story, God mocks evil. (No where is this more clear than at Calvary. Just as the Enemy believes he has carried the day, all his work is undone.) How is evil mocked in *The Count of Monte Cristo*? How have you seen evil mocked on your own journey?

NOTES

THE MYSTERY OF PAIN

FRAME

We've all asked those questions, but for all the answers the Christian faith provides about the origin of life, the reason for our existence, and the hope of our future, the subject of God and evil has always proven a thorny path for the contemplative heart. Is God all-powerful? Absolutely. Is He good? Of course. Then how do we explain the genocide of scores of innocent children in sub-Saharan Africa whose only apparent crime is to be born in the wrong place at the wrong time? Or, how do we make sense of a precious grandparent falling victim to Alzheimer's disease only to become a shadow of the person once known and loved?

Whether it's on the other side of the world or close to home, we struggle mightily as mere mortals with the mysterious ways of an eternal God. The quest is complex and impossible to travel alone. That's why, in this session, we will explore this rugged terrain of our faith together as we wrestle with why God sometimes chooses to prevent, sometimes chooses to intervene, but sometimes seems to do nothing at all.

1 WHAT IS ONE OF THE "HARD QUESTIONS" ABOUT LIFE THAT YOU WOULD LIKE TO ASK GOD?

2 GIVE ONE EXAMPLE FROM CURRENT EVENTS—GLOBALLY OR CLOSE TO HOME—THAT HAS RECENTLY GRABBED YOUR ATTENTION AND ILLUSTRATES HOW THE PROBLEM OF EVIL IS REAL.

CANVAS

Things happen for a reason... it's part of God's plan... Come again? How can this much loneliness and pain be part of God's plan? My friends tell me, "keep it together for the kids, take care of yourself, stay strong..." For the most part, I could put on a brave face. As long as there were tasks... and lists and schedules to keep. Sure, I'd hit a snag now and then. We might bump into someone, some well-meaning acquaintance who doesn't know what to say... with that look, that "Bless your heart" look. And then, in whispered tones reserved for those things sad and shameful, "I'm so sorry about you and Doug. How ARE you?"

But at sundown, slowdown, bedtime questions... why Mom? when Mom? Trying to answer honestly but leaving out the part about feeling scared. Sometimes, "I don't know" was the best I could muster. There were nights I could scarcely hold it all in until I tucked them in bed. I longed for the solace of my room, where I could finally let all the fear and loss just wash over and out. I know sometimes they could hear my sobs, but that's OK. Just as the mystery of pain eludes me, I can't fully grasp the mysteries of healing. I only know that Jesus has wept with me.

— MARY ANN —

PRIME

‹‹‹Show Video 6/6, Following You Thing›››

1. Pete suggests that there's something inside each of us that longs for meaning in the midst of pain and trauma. Are there currently some areas where you personally have been struggling to find meaning in the midst of pain?

2. To what do you attribute that longing within each of us? How do you think the longing with which we battle be God's way to draw us to Himself?

I think somewhere here in the mix of these questions is the desire for people to know if God still really cares. Yes, following God is hard. Yes, we are going to suffer in some way. Why? I don't know. But, answering the question "does God care?" helps me stay on the journey when the ups and downs come.

– BARRY –

3. Pete mentions that John the Baptist's question to Jesus in Matthew 11:3 could have been more of a statement: "I believe You are the One, but following You isn't turning out the way I thought it would." Does this statement resonate with you? How so?

4. Do you think we tend to avoid the big "Why?" questions? How do we avoid them? Why do you think it's difficult to "look this mystery in the eye"?

5. Pete said that we can be sure of two things: God's love and our suffering. How do these two truths, which seem so incapable of co-existing, actually connect the mystery of pain and the mystery of redemption quite seamlessly?

SKETCH

1. What are some clichés you often hear Christians use in an attempt to downplay the difficult questions about evil?

The mystery of God's ways in our world is not a new issue to the human race. Every generation has struggled to grasp how a loving deity and a broken world really works. From the greatest philosophers of old to the 4-year-old who screams, "that's not fair," the issue of what is right and what isn't has posed a challenge even to the most devout.

8"For My thoughts are not your thoughts, and your ways are not My ways." This is the Lord's declaration. 9"For as heaven is higher than earth, so My ways are higher than your ways, and My thoughts than your thoughts."   ISAIAH 55:8-9

We know that all things work together for the good of those who love God: those who are called according to His purpose.   ROMANS 8:28

---

2. One verse from the Old Testament, one from the New. Why do you think these verses are commonly used to address issues of evil?

3. Do you think the mystery of pain is easily solved? Audra sugggests that perhaps pain is necessary to appreciate what is good. Do you agree? Why or why not?

People here in the North talk about how much they love the seasons, how much more you appreciate the warmth of summer after enduring a bitter winter. I think that's crazy. Having grown up in the South, I can appreciate a nice warm day anytime. And if I never had to endure another day plagued with ice, below-zero temperatures, and several feet of snow I wouldn't mind in the least. Maybe pain is the same way. Maybe we need to undergo difficult times so that we appreciate the good times even more. Still, I wouldn't miss the painful experiences much either.

– AUDRA –

4. Do you believe that God has revealed enough about "His ways" to us in Scripture? Why or why not?

5. Why do you think God doesn't give us more "clues" as to what He is up to in our world, particularly as it relates to evil and pain?

For so long I bought into the idea of avoidance. You know, if it hurts get it to stop; do whatever you can to avoid pain. Treat everything with medication, whatever that may be—sports, activities, hobbies, anything that provides escape. For men it's called cave time. Then in an Isaac Newton moment I realized that pain and sickness and grief, they still happen; that cave time is just a way to avoid life. So if God allows pain, then there must be a reason. There must be something in those places for me to feel and become more whole through the feeling.

— BRIAN —

STRETCH

In our gut we know that life isn't easy. Our world tends to cheapen the human experience by convincing us that God is like a 30-minute sitcom with a beginning, middle, and end. So we rely on old clichés and quotes we've heard from someone else in an attempt to dull our pain and quiet our restless hearts. But instinctively we understand that there are moments of brutal honesty on the spiritual journey in which everything is not necessarily clear and not easily grasped.

"Keep asking, and it will be given to you. Keep searching, and you will find. Keep knocking, and the door will be opened to you. For everyone who asks receives, and the one who searches finds, and to the one who knocks, the door will be opened." **MATTHEW 7:7-8**

"Enter through the narrow gate. For the gate is wide and the road is broad that leads to destruction, and there are many who go through it. How narrow is the gate and difficult the road that leads to life, and few find it." **MATTHEW 7:13-14**

"When you come looking for me, you'll find me. Yes, when you get serious about finding me and want it more than anything else, I'll make sure you won't be disappointed." **JEREMIAH 29:13 (MSG)**

1. In what ways do you think our world discourages the process of honest "seeking"?

2. In the above passages Jesus reveals the brutally disruptive truth to our dream of happy endings for all: Everyone will not find Him. How do you think His listeners reacted to that teaching? What response do you have?

3. How would you describe the lifestyle of a person whose heart is set on seeking God?

4. If God is good and desires all people to be restored to a relationship with Him, then why would Jesus say that the gate is "narrow" and the road "difficult," with few finding true life?

While we would like to imagine a journey without heartache or pain, the reality is that seeking true answers often requires the courage to be led to wherever the answers may be found. Isaiah 42:16 refers to being led down "unfamiliar paths." While we may not be able to understand all that God is up to, we can begin to see how the clues are lining up. And in a fallen world, God's way is rarely discovered on the path of least resistance.

Honest seeking involves asking uncomfortable questions, or may even seem like you have doubt in God; which of course is not the case! Christianity in our time treats each question as if it has a logical answer that lines up in a neat systematic way. Do we honestly feel as if we have God totally figured out?

– DANIEL –

If God gives us all of the answers, then why seek Him out to learn more about Him? I like it that God doesn't give us all the answers. I feel like it is His way of saying that He wants us to experience the adventure of getting to know Him.

– DANIEL –

We also rejoice in our afflictions, because we know that affliction produces endurance, endurance produces proven character, and proven character produces hope. This hope does not disappoint, because God's love has been poured out in our hearts through the Holy Spirit who was given to us. ROMANS 5:3-5

During His earthly life, He offered prayers and appeals, with loud cries and tears, to the One who was able to save Him from death, and He was heard because of His reverence. Though a Son, He learned obedience through what He suffered. HEBREWS 5:7-8

Two years ago one of my friends found out she had breast cancer. It was a difficult battle, but now she is cancer free and speaks to grops as large as 2,000 with a message of encouragement drawn from her own story of survival. It reminds me that God does have the ability to make all things, even the painful ones, work together for good.

– AUDRA –

5. Why do you think hope birthed through suffering does not disappoint us, as Romans 5:3-5 says, when so much else does?

6. Why was it important for the writer of Hebrews to note what Jesus endured while on earth?

7. How does Jesus' example help you cope with the reality of the suffering around you?

The clues along our journeys begin to point us toward the reality that God allows situations and pain to bubble up to make us confront our shortcomings, to challenge our shallow thinking, and to lead us to a deeper place in relationship with Him. We were created to bear God's image, but in our most honest moments we realize that we're defaced masterpieces. Suffering so often provides the opportunity that God uses to drive us to surrender. In our bold stubbornness, we will pay attention no other way. As C.S. Lewis writes in *The Problem of Pain*: "God whispers to us in our pleasures, speaks in our conscience, but shouts in our pain: it is His megaphone to rouse a deaf world."[2]

---

[2] Page 91.

GLOSS

So what about the difficult relationship I am in? How about the child I know who is battling cancer? Why do thousands of children die every year when all they need is clean water? Our questions will never end in this lifetime. We'll always be haunted with the "why" issues of life because we are aliens and pilgrims in this strange land. And while our perspective in this life is drastically limited, through our relationship with God we discover that we have unprecedented access to a much higher vantage point.

Then Job replied to the Lord: "I know that you can do all things; no plan of yours can be thwarted. ... Surely I spoke of things I did not understand, things too wonderful for me to know."   *JOB 42:1-3 (NIV)*

"Be still, and know that I am God; I will be exalted among the nations, I will be exalted in the earth."   *PSALM 46:10 (NIV)*

"Call to Me and I will answer you and tell you great and wondrous things you do not know."   *JEREMIAH 33:3*

Let us then approach the throne of grace with confidence, so that we may receive mercy and find grace to help us in our time of need.   *HEBREWS 4:16 (NIV)*

There is possibly another side of this. There is the part about the battle over our hearts. It could be that much of the pain we feel results from being caught in the crossfire of this spiritual war that rages just on the other side of the curtain.

– BRIAN –

1. While there is no promise that we will avoid all pain, suffering, and encounters with evil in life, what provisions does God make for us?

2. When is a time in your life when you sensed God intervening on your behalf? Were you faithful to give God the credit?

3. What is an issue you are facing right now in which you desperately long for God's intervention? What clues do you have, if any, that He might be up to something through this experience?

4. How do you think God grieves with you in the pain and confusion of your life?

I think God grieves like any parent would grieve towards the hurt of their child. As I look at my 2 year old, any time that I see she may be lost, or confused in a situation, I'm already feeling extremely sad for her. I see the look on her face and it causes me to hurt, because all that I really want is for her to be protected.

– DANIEL –

Close in a time of group prayer, asking the Spirit to quiet your hearts so you can hear both His whispers to you and His cries of agony in your pain.

The Treatment Experience that follows is a group activity. Volunteer to host a final Bridge to process the conversations of the last several weeks.

CANVAS TREATMENT EXPERIENCE

We recommend getting the group together to a final discussion of these Mysteries. Early in the experience we talked about the empty canvas of our lives that awaits the first splashes of your own story. The last several weeks you have had the opportunity to brush the strokes of your journey on the canvas we have provided. Through this conversation you've engaged some of the more difficult and complex aspects of the Christian faith. Through it all we must understand that while theology has its place, God is so much bigger than any of our systems or methods of understanding. This experience has not been created to paint a more difficult picture of Who God is, but to paint a more amazing one. The big questions only serve to drive us deeper in relationship with one another and with God.

We recommend egg rolls. The recipe below makes a boatload. Use the questions here to drive the conversation as you put a wrap on this Canvas experience.

Egg Rolls

Ground beef, 1 lb.
Med. Onions, 2
Celery, 2 stalks
Cabbage (shredded), ½ head
Water chestnuts, 1 can
Egg roll wraps (2 pkg.)
Bean sprouts
Snow peas
Soy Sauce
Wok oil
Vegetable oil (or equivalent)
Salt
Pepper
Water, 1 c.

1. Brown ground beef in wok with salt, pepper, soy sauce, onion, and wok oil.
2. Add remaining ingredients and cook until vegetables are soft.
3. Heat vegetable oil in deep fryer.
4. Rub a small amount of flour on a cutting board so wraps will not stick.
5. Lay wrap on the board and, following directions on the package, wrap approximately two spoonfuls of the stir fry from the wok.
6. Use a little of the water to seal the egg roll before frying.
7. Repeat.

1.   What wounds has your story revealed?

2.   As you have mined the deepest places, what do you sense God is revealing to you? How do you think God wants to use the story He has been telling through you?

3.   What mystery is most captivating to you?

4.   Through this experience how have you begun to better understand or search your "internal world"?

5.   What has been the most profound revelation to you in the process of "painting" your own canvas?

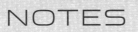

NOTES

NOTES

90/96

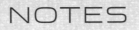

NOTES

CANVAS

A DVD-DRIVEN SMALL-GROUP EXPERIENCE.

Distortions, the first release from the Canvas series, identifies the ways our adversary has distorted reality. Distortions focuses on six areas: community, desire, self, world, God, and control—topics that lead to discussions about how each of these elements touches the story God is revealing through us. Using the power of story and art through DVD's and an Experience Guide for each group member, this small-group series brings a new multi-media dimension to Bible study.

Canvas: Distortions DVD Kit
1574943368

Canvas: Distortions Experience Guide
1574943375

FOUNDATIONS

EXPERIENCE THE MYSTERY FOR THE FIRST TIME. AGAIN.

Jesus seemed to love paradox and often taught by asking questions rather than dumping information. It's an idea we can all connect with—an idea we all struggle with. At some point in our lives, we've had questions—"Who is God" and "Where was He when..." God can handle these questions and desires the intimacy that comes from working through them. *The Foundations of the Faith* series takes groups through this process.

Foundational Truths
1574943111

Knowing Jesus
1574943103

The Christian in a Postmodern World
1574941089

God and the Journey to Truth
1574941097

GOD & THE ARTS

WHERE FAITH INTERSECTS LIFE.

Stories, great and small, share the same essential structure because every story we tell borrows its power from a Larger Story. What we sense stirring within is a heart that is made for a place in the Larger Story. It is no accident that great movies include a hero, a villain, a betrayal, a battle to fight, a romance, and a beauty to rescue. It is The Epic story and it is truer than anything we know. Adventure awaits. Listen.

Discover an experience that guides you on a journey into the one great Epic in which the Bible is set. This fun and provocative study features four films, each with two small-group meetings, *Dinner and a Movie* (Week 1), *Connecting the Dots* (Week 2), and an *Experience Guide* that offers valuable insights.

Finding Jesus in the Movies
1574943553

Finding Redemption in the Movies
1574943421

LEADING A SMALL-GROUP EXPERIENCE

You will find a great deal of information in this section that is crucial to success in leading the Canvas Experience.

Reading through this and utilizing the suggested principles and practices will greatly enhance the group experience. You need to accept the limitations of leadership. You cannot transform a life. You must lead your group to the Bible and the power of the Holy Spirit. By doing so, you are giving your group the tools necessary to experience Canvas.

SETTING THE ENVIRONMENT

GENERAL TIPS:

1. Prepare for each meeting by reviewing the material, praying for each group member, and asking the Holy Spirit to join you at each meeting. Make Jesus the centerpiece of every experience.
2. Create the right environment by making sure chairs are arranged so each person can see the eyes of every other attendee. Set the room temperature at 69 degrees. Request that cell phones be turned off unless someone is expecting an emergency call. Have music playing as people arrive. Create a fun and inviting atmosphere.
3. Try to have soft drinks and water available for early arrivals.
4. Have people with the spiritual gift of hospitality ready to make any new attendees feel welcome.
5. Be sure there is adequate lighting so that everyone can read without straining.
6. Four types of questions are used in each session: Observation (What is the passage telling us?), Interpretation (What does the passage mean?), Self-revelation (How am I doing in light of the truth unveiled?), and Application (Now that I know what I know, what will I do to integrate this truth into my life?). You won't be able to use all the questions in each study, but be sure to use some of each throughout the CANVAS experience.
7. Connect with group members outside of meeting time.
8. Don't get impatient about the depth of spiritual growth group members seem to be experiencing. Real change at a heart level takes time.
9. Be sure pens and/or pencils are available for attendees at each meeting.
10. Never ask someone to pray aloud without first getting his or her permission.

EVERY MEETING:

1. Before starting a DVD, do not say, "Now we're going to watch a video." Instead, initiate the segment by telling the group a little bit about what to look for. The meeting should feel like a conversation from beginning to end—not a classroom experience.

2. Create a sense of engagement and interaction through your time together.

3. Remember, a great group leader talks less than 10% of the time. If you ask a question and no one answers, wait. If you create an environment where you fill the gaps of silence, the group will quickly learn they needn't join you in the conversation.

4. If members are hesitant, draw attention to something from the video or from sidebar Canvas pieces.

5. Don't be hesitant to call people by name as you ask them to respond to questions or to give their opinions. Be sensitive, but engage everyone in the conversation.

REMEMBER:

Each small group has its own persona. Every group is made up of a unique set of personalities, backgrounds, and life experiences. This diversity creates a dynamic distinctive to a specific group of people. Embracing the unique character of your group and the individuals in it is vital to helping group members experience all you're hoping for.

Treat each person as a special, responsible, and valued member of the group. By doing so you'll bring out the best in each of them, while creating a living, breathing, life-changing group dynamic.

Acknowledgments

Publisher
Ron Keck

Project Manager and General Editor
Brian Daniel

Art Director
Brian Marschall

Host
Pete Wilson

Creative Direction
Pete Wilson
Brian Daniel
Jenni Catron
Matt Singleton

Experience Guide
Jay Strother
Brian Daniel
Barry Cram
Wendi Zebell
Justine Scheriger

Manufacturing
Royce Armstrong
Lynn Newcomb
Sherry Turrentine

Canvas is produced in partnership with *Refined. Refined* is a non-profit ministry organization developed to create cutting-edge, culturally relevant media elements and resources. Founded by Pete Wilson, Senior Pastor of Cross Point Community Church in Nashville, TN, *Refined* specializes in video teaching segments that can be used in church services, small group discussions, personal discipleship and more.